Thumb Position

for Cello
Book 2

"Thumbs of Steel"

by Rick Mooney

Alfred Music
P.O. Box 10003
Van Nuys, CA 91410-0003
alfred.com

ISBN-10: 0-87487-764-4
ISBN-13: 978-0-87487-764-9

About the Author

Rick Mooney grew up in a musical family where he began studying piano at the age of five and cello at the age of eight. He studied both instruments until high school graduation when he decided to concentrate on the cello while he took a degree in mathematics at the University of Southern California. He studied with Gabor Rejto and Eleanore Schoenfeld while attending USC. He studied Suzuki teaching methods at USC with Phyllis Glass and studied in Japan in the spring of 1976. Mr. Mooney teaches cello privately in the Los Angeles area. He has played with many performing groups throughout southern California and currently plays in the professional cello quartet, "Quatracelli!" He has also performed as soloist with the Claremont Community Orchestra and the Claremont Chamber Orchestra.

Mr. Mooney is the founder and director of the National Cello Institute, which has held a week-long session each summer since 1976. The National Cello Institute also holds an annual Winter Suzuki Cello Workshop.

As a specialist in the Suzuki method of teaching, he has been active with the Suzuki Association of the Americas, serving on the Board of Directors, on the Cello Committee and writing for the American Suzuki Journal. He has been invited to teach at many institutes, conferences and workshops throughout the United States, as well as in Canada, England, Australia, Japan, Korea and Taiwan.

Contents

A Note to Students

Perhaps the first thing I should emphasize is that the subtitle of this book, "Thumbs of Steel," is used in fun. You should not conclude that there should be anything stiff or inflexible about your thumb when you use it on the cello. In fact, your hand should be heavy with the balanced weight from your back, but the whole hand should remain round and flexible. So with that disclaimer out of the way...

It is assumed that before you begin this book you are completely familiar with the four basic thumb position finger patterns. This book expands on that foundation. The book is organized as follows:

- The section of the book introduced by Daily Warm-ups — Group 1 uses mainly a chromatic fingering pattern.

- The section of the book introduced by Daily Warm-ups — Group 2 deals with extension of the hand, where the thumb remains in place and the hand opens and closes as necessary.

- The section of the book introduced by Daily Warm-ups — Group 3 requires that the thumb move across to the G-string periodically.

- The section of the book introduced by Daily Warm-ups — Group 4 requires that the hand move in and out of thumb position.

Until this point in the book, the thumb plays on the half-string harmonics. The entire remainder of the book deals with moving the thumb off of that spot. This is presented in a logical way (beginning with Daily Warm-ups — Group 5) using the harmonics as "targets" to set the hand in the required places. Here are a few things to think about in the last half of the book:

Because the thumb has been on the harmonic spot, it has been optional to stop the strings solidly with the thumb. Now it will be required that you "sink" the weight from your back into the strings and play solid notes without causing any collapse or tension in the knuckles. With my own students, I don't wait until now to practice this idea. I ask that my students play their thumb solidly on the A-string from the beginning of the book — even when that note is a harmonic. In this way, we get used to being firm and flexible at the same time so that when we must also stop the D-string firmly, it is not such a big adjustment.

Since the thumb will be moving all over the fingerboard, you must now be more careful to notice the specific placement of your hand. Here are a few hints:

- I have tried to help you by occasionally indicating which string you should be on (I is the A-string, II is the D-string, etc.).

- Once you have your thumb set in the proper place, you must also know what notes are available to your fingers in that particular spot. Once you move off the harmonic spot, certain fingerings that may seem automatic to you will no longer work, so pay attention!

- I ask my students to "know the facts." By this I mean that they must know the specific names of the notes to be played and the distances between those notes. In this way, they can consciously choose the correct fingering pattern for each circumstance.

- I have always marked a fingering for you if a shift is required. So you should assume that if you do not see a fingering, you do not have to shift. In these places you must figure out how to play the notes without moving your hand.

A few words about the Daily Warm-ups:

Please play all of the Daily Warm-ups. You will find that in addition to preparing you for the pieces in this book, there are excerpts you will find useful in other places in the future. You need not do all of the warm-ups before beginning the pieces, but do a couple each day until they are all covered.

In several places you will see two sets of slur marks. The intention here is that you should begin the exercise slowly with fewer notes per bow. As you get comfortable with the exercise, then you should play more quickly with the longer slurs.

My students and I have had a lot of fun with the pieces in this book. I hope you, too, find this a pleasant way to develop your thumb position technique. Enjoy!

— Rick Mooney

Daily Warm-ups -- Group 1

March of the Wooden Soldiers

Tempo di Marcia

P. I. Tchaikowsky

March of the Wooden Soldiers

Around the Gypsy Campfire

Rick Mooney

Around the Gypsy Campfire

Harry the Hirsute Housefly

Rick Mooney

Harry the Hirsute Housefly

* slap (swat) the fingerboard with the palm of your right hand

Harry the Hirsute Housefly

Daily Warm-ups -- Group 2

In each of these warm-ups, leave your thumb in its place and open (extend) your hand as necessary.

Daily Warm-ups -- Group 2 continued

The Drummers

The Drummers

The Drummers

Loch Leven Castle

Petite Partita

Rick Mooney

22

Petite Partita

Petite Partita

Daily Warm-ups -- Group 3

In each of these warm-ups, move your thumb across strings when marked with *

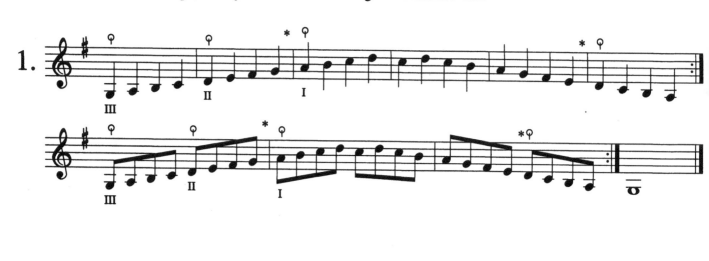

The Sailor and His Girlfriend

Fine

The Sailor and His Girlfriend

D. S. al Fine

The Rollicking Irishman

The Rollicking Irishman

Fine

The Rollicking Irishman

D. S. al Fine

Daily Warm-ups -- Group 4

Chorale
Ich Freue Mich In Dir

J. S. Bach

Aria

Anna Magdalena Notebook

Two Irish Jigs

Fine

Two Irish Jigs

D. S. al Fine

Clydesdale Lasses

Clydesdale Lasses

Daily Warm-ups -- Group 5

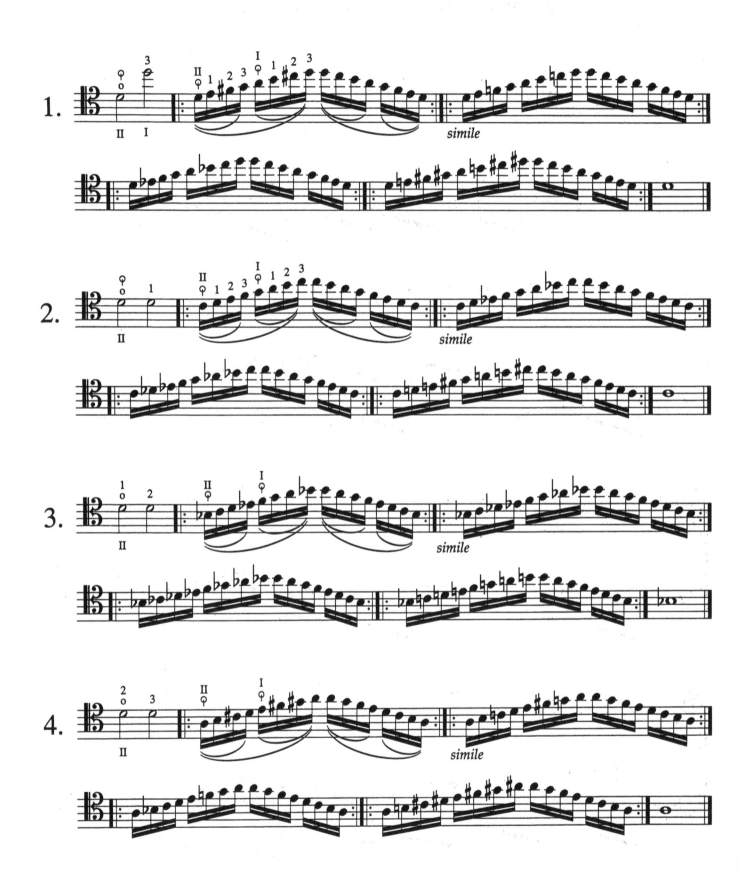

Moon Over the Ruined Castle

R. Taki

Flora MacDonald

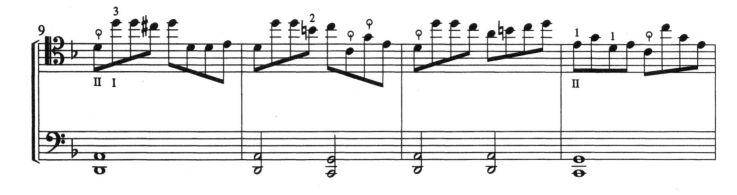

Soldier's Joy

Daily Warm-ups -- Group 6

3.

4.

Michael, Row the Boat Ashore

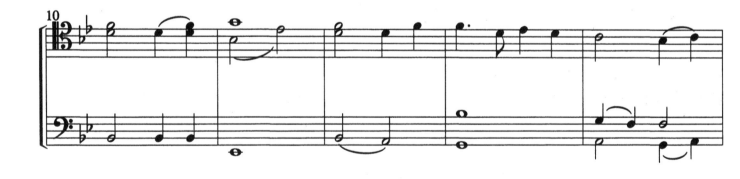

Michael, Row the Boat Ashore

The Unfortunate Rake

Maytime

W. A. Mozart

48

Timour the Tarter

Fine

D. S. al Fine

Daily Warm-ups -- Group 7

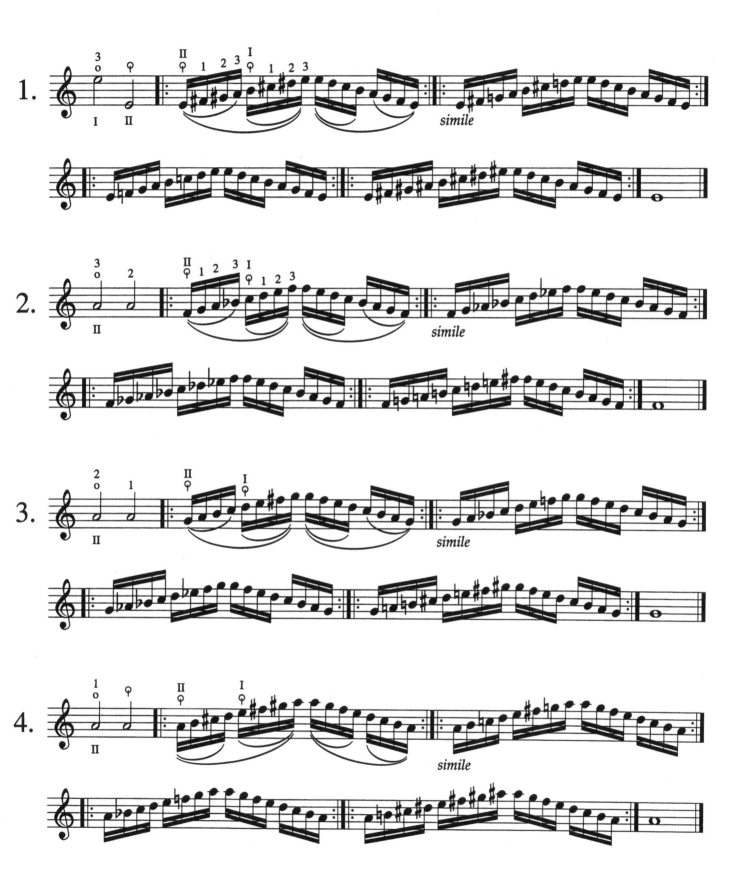

Mrs. McLeod

The Devil Among the Tailors

Believe Me, If All Those
Endearing Young Charms

Yankee Doodle

Daily Warm-ups -- Group 8

1.

2.

Scottish Tune

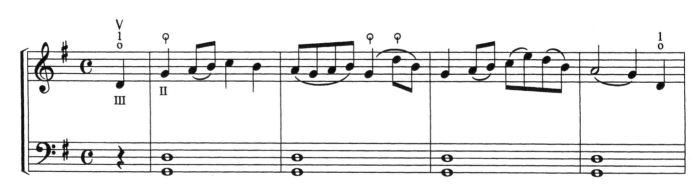

Larry Grogan

58

Camptown Races

Stephen Foster

My Home Away From Home

Rick Mooney

Daily Warm-ups -- Group 9

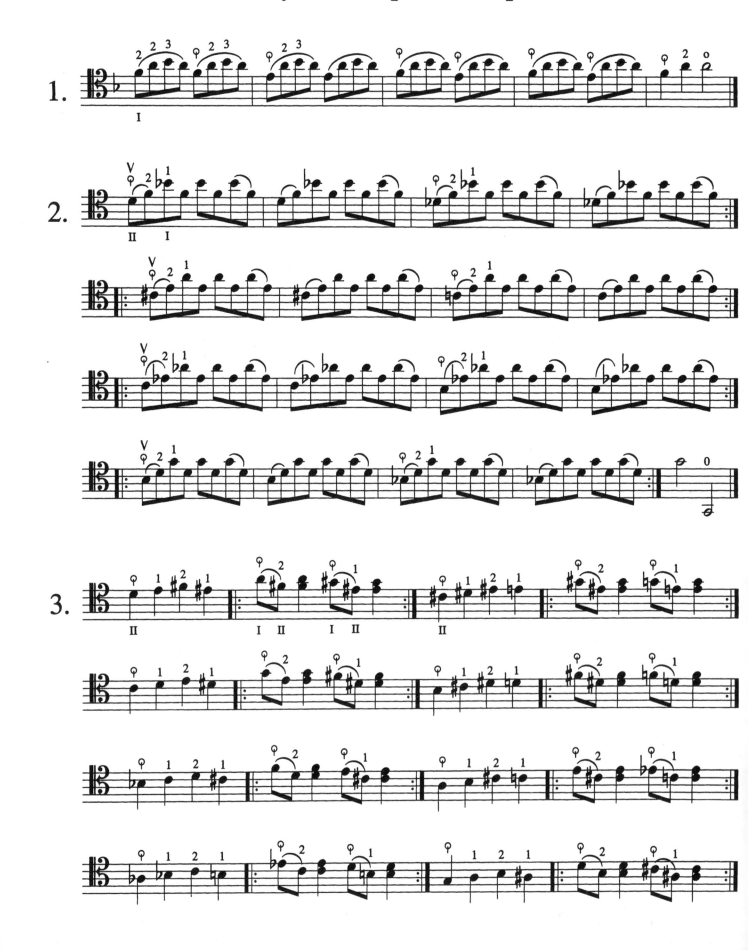

Daily Warm-ups -- Group 10

The Spinning Wheel

Rick Mooney

The Spinning Wheel

Cajun Waltz

Rick Mooney

Cajun Waltz

Daily Warm-ups -- Group 11

Carolan's Quarrel

Turlough O'Carolan

sempre pizz.

Carolan's Quarrel

D. S. al Coda

⊕ Coda

I Dream of You
Through the Endless Night

Rick Mooney

sempre pizz.

Fine

I Dream of You

D. S. al Fine

Daily Warm-ups -- Group 12

Daily Warm-ups -- Group 13

Thumb Callous Blues

Rick Mooney

Thumb Callous Blues

* Strum (pizz.) back and forth with thumb

Blue Ridge Ballad

Rick Mooney

Blue Ridge Ballad

D. C. al Fine

Chromatic Boogie

Rick Mooney

Chromatic Boogie